THE LITTLE GUIDE TO

FREDDIE
MERCURY

MIX
Paper | Supporting
responsible forestry
FSC® C020056

Published in 2023 by OH!
An Imprint of Welbeck Non-Fiction Limited,
part of Welbeck Publishing Group.
Offices in: London – 20 Mortimer Street, London W1T 3JW
and Sydney – Level 17, 207 Kent St, Sydney NSW 2000 Australia
www.welbeckpublishing.com

ISBN 978-1-80069-549-8

Compiled and written by: Isobel Stewart
Editorial: Ann Reid
Project manager: Russell Porter
Design: Tony Seddon
Production: Jess Brisley

A CIP catalogue record for this book is available from the British Library

Printed in China

10 9 8 7 6 5 4 3 2 1

THE LITTLE GUIDE TO
FREDDIE MERCURY

THE SHOW MUST GO ON

OH!

CONTENTS

INTRODUCTION

A groundbreaking songwriter, consummate entertainer and one of the 20th century's most iconic performers, Freddie Mercury fronted Queen from 1970 until his death in 1991. With his incredible vocal range, flamboyant stage presence and captivating personality, he remains one of the most recognized figures in the history of rock music.

Throughout his career, the singer was known for his powerful and emotive voice and his charismatic persona. He wrote many of Queen's most popular and enduring songs, including "Bohemian Rhapsody", "We Are the Champions" and "Don't Stop Me Now", which continue to resonate with audiences around the world. And never afraid to take musical risks, he challenged many of the prevailing pop and rock parameters.

But alongside his astonishing skill as a musician, Freddie is equally remembered for his masterful stagecraft and ability to command an audience. Queen's appearance at the Live Aid Concert at London's Wembley Stadium in July 1985 remains one of the most incredible rock performances of all time.

Beyond his musical accomplishments, the singer was an inspirational trailblazer for the LGBTQ+ community. He fearlessly defied societal norms and stereotypes, particularly with his flamboyant fashion sense and openly gay identity at a time when it was still considered taboo. And, in the face of his AIDS diagnosis, his unapologetic authenticity inspired – and continues to inspire – millions.

Packed full of fabulous quotes – from Freddie himself, but also from bandmates, friends and fellow musicians – as well as fascinating facts about his life and career, this little guide is a wonderful celebration of the Queen frontman. From his wit and humour to his passion and drive, it offers a glimpse into the mind and heart of one of the greatest performers of all time.

CHAPTER
ONE

THE GREAT PRETENDER

The Real Freddie...

In 1987, Freddie Mercury recorded "The Great Pretender". The Queen frontman once said, "Most of the stuff I do is pretending. It's like acting…"

Freddie was an enigma. Famous for his flamboyant showmanship and the way he commanded a stage, he was one of the rock world's most magnetic performers. Yet, in private, he was a shy and introverted character – and someone who fiercely guarded his privacy.

> **"**
>
> I'm not going to be a star, I'm going to be a legend! I want to be the Rudolf Nureyev of rock 'n' roll.
>
> **"**

Freddie Mercury: A Life, In His Own Words,
September 2019

"

Some people can take second best, but I can't. If you've got the taste for being number one, then number two isn't good enough.

"

In an interview with David Wigg, as quoted on Mail Online, 18 February 2011

Freddie Mercury was born
Farrokh Bulsara in Stone Town,
Zanzibar (now Tanzania).
His parents were Parsees –
followers of the Zoroastrian
religion – from western India.

He grew up in Zanzibar
and India before moving to
Middlesex, England when
he was a teenager.

❝

I was a precocious child. My parents thought boarding school would do me good so they sent me to one when I was seven, dear. I look back on it and I think it was marvellous. You learn to look after yourself and it taught me to have responsibility.

❞

In an interview with Caroline Coon, "The Queen Bee", *Melody Maker*, December 1974

66

I was a very insecure young
boy, probably because
I was a bit sheltered.

99

Freddie Mercury: A Life, In His Own Words,
September 2019

66

I was quite rebellious,
and my parents hated it.
I grew out of living at home
at an early age. But I just
wanted the best. I wanted
to be my own boss.

99

"Queen Holds Court in South America",
Rolling Stone, 11 June 1981

66

If I have time, [I spend a lot of time in front of the mirror]. I'm a very vain person...

99

"Queen's Freddie Mercury Shopping for an Image in London", *Circus Magazine*, April 1975

66

Our academic qualifications didn't help us with rock. As far as I was concerned, I was an art school reject who had a diploma in graphics, but how did that qualify me for rock? But what it did, having that background, was help us in the art of survival in the business side.

99

"The Man Who Would Be Queen", *Melody Maker*, 2 May 1981

"

There are times when
I wake up and think,
'My God! I wish I wasn't
Freddie Mercury today.'

"

Freddie Mercury: A Life, In His Own Words,
September 2019

"
I'm just a musical prostitute,
my dear. I'm just me.
"

TV interview, Munich, 1984

At the age of eight, Mercury was sent to a British-style boarding school near Bombay (now Mumbai), where he adopted the name "Freddie".

A fan of western pop music, he and four friends formed a school band called The Hectics, covering music by the likes of Little Richard and Elvis Presley.

66

Freddie was very shy, but once he started playing his piano, he became a completely different person. But I don't remember him as being any kind of showman – not at that age, anyway.

99

Victory Rana, former bandmate from Freddie's school band, The Hectics

66

I'd be doing myself an injustice if I didn't wear makeup because some people think it's wrong. Even to talk about being gay used to be obnoxious and unheard of. But gone are those days. There's a lot of freedom today and you can put yourself across anyway you want to. But I haven't chosen this image. I'm myself and in fact half the time I let the wind take me.

99

In an interview with Caroline Coon, "The Queen Bee", *Melody Maker*, 21 December 1974

"

People are apprehensive
when they meet me and they
think I'm going to eat them.
But underneath it all I'm quite
shy and very few people know
what I'm really like.

"

As quoted in an article on recordcollectormag.com,
15 October 2007

66

Most of the stuff I do is
pretending. It's like acting.
So you go on stage, and
I pretend to be a macho
man and all that. And in
my videos, you go through
all the different characters
– and you're pretending.

99

Final filmed interview, with Rudi Dolezal, early 1987

66
No, Mercury isn't my real name, dear. I changed it from Pluto.
99

In an interview with Caroline Coon, "The Queen Bee",
Melody Maker, 21 December 1974

Freddie's incredible voice had a range of almost four octaves, which he attributed to his protruding teeth.

He had four extra incisors, and although he was self-conscious about his overbite – he endured the nickname of "Bucky" at school – he thought that correcting his teeth would affect his vocal range.

"

Escalating within a few bars from a deep, throaty rock-growl to tender, vibrant tenor, then on to a high-pitched, perfect coloratura, pure and crystalline in the upper reaches...

"

Biographer David Bret describes Freddie's voice,
Freddie Mercury: The Biography, 2016

"

I play on the bisexual thing because it's something else, it's fun. But I don't put on the show because I feel I have to and the last thing I want to do is give people an idea of exactly who I am. I want people to work out their own interpretation of me and my image. I don't want to build a frame around myself and say, 'This is what I am' or 'This is all I am.'

"

As quoted in Benoît Clerc, *Queen: All the Songs – The Story Behind Every Track*, 2019

66

There are very few people, basically people who I call very close friends, who actually know the other side of me… But there are two sides to me, you know, I think there's many sides to most people.

99

Interview with Simon Bates, BBC Radio 1, June 1985

"

Listening to Jimi Hendrix; Liza Minnelli; going to art galleries. I like most of the Victorian artists. I like a lot of detail work, water colours, that sort of thing. And popular stuff like Dali.

"

On being asked what his favourite form of entertainment was, "Queen's Freddie Mercury Shopping for an Image in London", *Circus Magazine*, April 1975

66

Can you imagine how terrible it is when you've got everything and you're still desperately lonely? That is awful beyond words.

99

As quoted in "Rock on, Freddie", *Sunday Magazine*, May 1985

In 1966, Freddie began studying art and graphic design at Ealing Art College in London.

He later put his artistic talents to good use when he designed Queen's famous logo, shortly before the release of the band's debut album in 1973.

It combines the zodiac signs of the four members – two lions for Leo (Taylor and Deacon), a crab for Cancer (May), and two fairies for Virgo (Mercury).

"

Back then, I didn't really know him as a singer — he was just my mate. My crazy mate! If there was fun to be had, Freddie and I were usually involved.

"

Roger Taylor, recalling his early friendship with Freddie

66

I'm a flamboyant personality. I like going out and having a good time. I'm just being me.

99

"Queen Holds Court in South America", *Rolling Stone*, 11 June 1981

66

Every time I'm in the same room with Brian, within five minutes we sort of start [to fight]. I haven't hit him yet … but there's still time!

99

In an interview with Lisa Robinson, 1984

❝

It's very hard to find friends – to have loyal friends and to keep them. Among my friends are a lot of gay people and a lot of girls and a lot of old men. The man I have as a chauffeur – we've, built up such a bond, it's a kind of love, and I don't care what people think about it.

❞

"In an interview with Caroline Coon, "The Queen Bee", *Melody Maker*, 21 December 1974

"

To be honest, not much embarrasses me actually. It's not embarrassment, but maybe annoyance, that I feel when things aren't going right onstage.

"

"Queen's Freddie Mercury Shopping for an Image in London", *Circus Magazine*, April 1975

66

I have a lot of sex. Try and get out of that one!

99

On being asked about his hobbies, television interview, Leiden, 1984

66

If I had to do this every day, forget it!

99

On being asked how he felt about press interviews, Munich, 1984

CHAPTER
TWO

LOVE OF MY LIFE

Freddie, the Romantic...

Freddie's longest relationship was with Mary Austin, for whom he is said to have written the ballad "Love of my Life". He also had relationships with several men, including Jim Hutton, whom he remained with until his death in 1991.

Freddie once spoke of how he was "possessed by love" – and indeed, love, yearning and loss were themes that poignantly featured in many of Queen's songs.

66

I can't win. Love is Russian roulette for me. No one loves the real me inside. They're all in love with my fame, my stardom.

99

As quoted in "Rock on, Freddie", *Sunday Magazine*, May 1985

"

A song can mean anything.
But I'm a true romantic
and a very loving person,
and I think that comes out
in my songs.

"

Press conference, 1985

In his twenties, Freddie began singing in various bands in London – Ibex, Wreckage and Sour Milk Sea – and sold vintage clothes in London's Kensington Market with his friend Roger Taylor. In 1970, he joined forces with drummer Taylor and guitarist Brian May to become lead singer of their group, Smile. Bassist John Deacon joined the lineup in 1971.

Freddie soon changed his surname from Bulsara to Mercury, and persuaded his bandmates to change the group's name. At a show in Truro on 27 June 1970, the band announced themselves as Queen.

66

[The name 'Queen' is] very regal obviously, and it sounds splendid. It's a strong name, very universal and immediate. I was certainly aware of the gay connotations, but that was just one facet of it.

99

As quoted in "Who was Freddie Mercury?", *Seattle Gay News*, vol. 33, no. 36, 9 September 2005

"
I'm very emotional;
I think I may go mad in
several years' time.

"

Circus magazine, 17 March 1977

Six Love Songs

Love of my Life, 1975

Good Old-Fashioned
Lover Boy, 1976

Somebody to Love, 1976

Crazy Little Thing Called
Love, 1980

Love Kills, 1984

I Was Born to Love You, 1985

66

In terms of love, you're not in control and I hate that feeling. I seem to write a lot of sad songs because I'm a very tragic person. But there's always an element of humour at the end.

99

As quoted in "I am the Champion" by Nick Ferrari, *The Sun*, 19 July 1985

> **❝**
> Over the years I have
> become bitter and I don't
> trust anybody because
> they've let me down...
> **❞**

Interview with David Wigg, 1985

66

I am a romantic, but I do put up a barrier around myself, so it is hard for people to get in and to know the real me. I fall in love much too quickly and that results in me getting badly hurt. The problem with love is that you lose control and that is a very vulnerable state to be in.

99

Article by Emma Powys Maurice, posted on thepinknews.com, 24 November 2021

66

Our love affair ended in tears but a deep bond grew out of it, and that's something nobody can take away from us. It's unreachable...

99

On Mary Austin, as quoted in "Rock on, Freddie",
Sunday Magazine, May 1985

"

All my lovers asked me why they couldn't replace Mary, but it's simply impossible. The only friend I've got is Mary and I don't want anybody else. To me, [Mary] was my common-law wife. To me, it was a marriage. We believe in each other, that's enough for me.

"

On Mary Austin, as quoted in "For A Song: The Mercury that's rising in rock is Freddie, the satiny seductor of Queen" by Fred Hauptfuhrer, *People* magazine, 5 December 1977

66

I don't feel jealous of [Mary's] lovers because of course, she has a life to lead, and so do I. Basically, I try to make sure she's happy with whoever she's with and she tries to do the same for me. We look after each other and that's a wonderful form of love.
I might have all the problems in the world, but I have Mary and that gets me through.

99

On Mary Austin, as quoted in "Rock on, Freddie", *Sunday Magazine*, May 1985

Queen released their first album, *Queen*, in 1973. It was soon followed by a second album, *Queen II*, in 1974, which included the hit single "Seven Seas of Rhye".

Rhye was a fantasy world that Freddie dreamed up with his sister, Kashimara Bulsara, when they were children. Several other of the singer's early songs feature the mysterious land of Rhye, including "Lily of the Valley" and "My Fairy King".

66

My lyrics are basically for people's interpretations really. I've forgotten what they were all about. It's really factitious... It's just a figment of your imagination... I find [lyrics] quite a task and my strongest point is actually melody content. I concentrate on that first; melody, then the song structure, then the lyrics come after, actually.

99

BBC Radio One, 24 December 1977

"

My dearest, I'm sorry about last night but that's because I'm a dreadful tart! – Love you with all my heart – Kisses – Mercles xx.

"

Postcard to his first boyfriend, David Minns, 1975

66

You can have everything in the world and still be the loneliest man. And that is the most bitter type of loneliness, success has brought me world idolization and millions of pounds. But it's prevented me from having the one thing we all need: a loving, ongoing relationship.

99

As quoted in "Rock on, Freddie", *Sunday Magazine*, May 1985

"

I've stopped going out, stopped the nights of wild partying. I thought sex was important to me, but now I've gone the other way. What more can I do? I've stopped having sex and started growing tulips.

"

As quoted in an article on recordcollectormag.com, 15 October 2007

66

I would love to really have a beautiful relationship with somebody, but it never seems to work out. What I would like most of all is to be in a state of blissful love.

99

Article by Emma Powys Maurice, posted on thepinknews.com, 24 November 2021

Sheer Heart Attack was released in 1975, giving Queen its first international hit, "Killer Queen".

Penned by Freddie, the song is about a high-class call girl and was described as the beginning of Queen's "radio sound". Unusually, Freddie wrote the lyrics before the melody – normally, he would do the opposite.

66

People are used to hard rock, energy music from Queen, yet with this single you almost expect Noël Coward to sing it. It's one of those bowler hat, black suspender belt numbers – not that Coward would wear that.

99

NME, 2 November 1974

CHAPTER
THREE

WE WILL ROCK YOU

Freddie, the Rock Star...

As a child in India, Freddie developed a love of western pop music, but his influences were many. Taking inspiration from rockstars such as David Bowie, showbiz greats like Liza Minelli and opera stars such as Pavarotti, the Queen frontman shifted between different genres with ease.

As his unique sound and incredible style of performance developed, Freddie became a rock star in every sense of the word.

"

When I was a small child, in the choir in India, I just loved to sing. Then I realized I could actually write songs and make my own music. It dawned on me that I could do it my way. Suddenly there was a little taste of success, and I liked it.

"

As quoted in an article on recordcollectormag.com, 15 October 2007

66

I'm one of those people
who believes in doing those
things which interest you.
Music is so interesting, dear.

99

In an interview with Caroline Coon, "The Queen Bee",
Melody Maker, 21 December 1974

In 1975, the epic single "Bohemian Rhapsody", from the album *A Night at the Opera*, was released.

Its audacious operatic style and length – five minutes and 53 seconds – meant that it nearly never saw radio play, but it was an instant hit.

It became the UK Christmas number one, holding the top spot for nine weeks.

66

I remember Freddie coming in with loads of bits of paper from his dad's work, like post-it notes, and pounding on the piano… He played the piano like most people play the drums. And this song he had was full of gaps where he explained that something operatic would happen here and so on. He'd worked out the harmonies in his head.

99

Brian May recalls hearing an early working of "Bohemian Rhapsody", as quoted on udiscovermusic.com, 20 November 2022

"

The idea of Queen was conceived by me whilst I was studying in college…
Brian who was also at college liked the idea and we joined forces.

"

"Standing up for Queen", *Melody Maker*, 28 July 1973

"

It's my work, and I'm very serious about it, getting it right – when we began, we approached it the way we did because we were not prepared to be out-of-work musicians, ever. We said either take it on as a serious commodity or don't do it at all.

"

"The Man Who Would Be Queen", *Melody Maker*, 2 May 1981

"

I think we know now instinctively what each other wants. We go our separate ways. We have four limousines waiting after each show and we just go wherever we want. It's like a job, as I say. Your come together, do a gig...

"

On being asked whether the group socialized, "The Man Who Would Be Queen", *Melody Maker*, 2 May 1981

66

Jimi Hendrix is very important. He's my idol. He sort of epitomizes, from his presentation on stage, the whole works of a rock star. There's no way you can compare him. You either have the magic or you don't. There's no way you can work up to it. There's nobody who can take his place.

99

As quoted in "Queen's Freddie Mercury Shopping for an Image in London", *Circus Magazine*, April 1975

At the age of 24, Freddie met 19-year-old Mary Austin. Love blossomed, and the couple moved into a cramped flat near Kensington Market. In 1973, Freddie proposed to her – although they never actually married.

After the singer's homosexuality became apparent, the pair separated in 1976. However, they remained very close for the rest of his life, with Freddie leaving half his £75million estate, royalties and Kensington mansion to Austin.

66

All my lovers asked me why they couldn't replace Mary, but it's simply impossible. The only friend I've got is Mary, and I don't want anybody else. To me, she was my common-law wife. To me, it was a marriage.

99

As quoted in "For A Song: The Mercury that's rising in rock is Freddie, the satiny seductor of Queen" by Fred Hauptfuhrer, *People* magazine, 5 December 1977

66

I think Queen songs are pure escapism, like going to see a good film – after that, people can go away, and go back to their problems.

99

"The Man Who Would Be Queen", *Melody Maker*, 2 May 1981

66

I've got this idea for a song.

99

As quoted by producer Roy Thomas Baker, recalling
Freddie's introduction to "Bohemian Rhapsody"

As a child, Freddie avidly collected stamps, many from British Commonwealth territories. In 1993, his collection was acquired by the British Postal Museum, with proceeds going to the HIV/AIDS charity Mercury Phoenix Trust, which was started in his honour.

Even as a stamp collector, Freddie was unconventional: on some album pages, the stamps were ordered by colour or size. On others, patterns were created, or letters from the alphabet were formed.

"

I think I'm totally original.
I'm sure there are many
people who see themselves
in me, but that's to them.
I'm me, basically, and
that's how I like to be.

"

"Queen's Freddie Mercury Shopping for an Image in London", *Circus Magazine*, April 1975

66

It's going to be Number One for centuries.

99

BBC DJ Kenny Everett after hearing
"Bohemian Rhapsody" for the first time, 1975

66

A lot of people slammed 'Bohemian Rhapsody', but who can you compare that to? Name one group that's done an operatic single.

99

Circus magazine, 17 March 1977

❝

I'll say no more than what any decent poet would tell you if you dared ask him to analyze his work: 'If you see it, dear, then it's there.'

❞

On being asked to explain the meaning of "Bohemian Rhapsody", 1975

"

This is our music and it's up to the individual to interpret it. It's not up to us to come out with a product and label it. It would be boring if everything was laid out and everybody knew what it was all about all the time. I like people to make up their interpretation.

"

Interview with Harvey Kubernik, 1975

"

For me [Freddie] represents an era when people were less afraid of living life to the full. This was in the seventies, when rock's extravagances went beserk. Perhaps we're not living in that time any more. There's a glorious rebelliousness about it, of freedom attached to it, that represents that whole spirit of rock 'n' roll.

"

Annie Lennox, as quoted on freddiemercury.com

66

We're perfectionists. Although all of us write, it doesn't necessarily mean that every song composed will appear on an album. Having all the members write adds to our versatility, and that's another strong point.

99

Interview with Harvey Kubernik, 1975

"

Rock and roll has a very wide spectrum and you can do anything you want in it.

"

Radio 1990, February 1984

"

The whole group aimed for the top slot. We're not going to be content with anything less. That's what we're striving for. It's got to be there. I definitely know we've got it in the music, we're original enough... and, now we're proving it.

"

In an interview with Caroline Coon, "The Queen Bee", *Melody Maker*, 21 December 1974

In the 1970s, hit singles such as "Bohemian Rhapsody", "We Are the Champions" and "We Will Rock You" sealed Queen's reputation as a world-wide phenomenon.

In 2011, "We are the Champions", written by Freddie, was hailed as the catchiest song in the history of pop music, despite its not reaching number one in any major market.

"

I was thinking about football when I wrote it. I wanted a participation song, something that the fans could latch on to. It was aimed at the masses; I thought we'd see how they took it... Of course, I've given it more theatrical subtlety than an ordinary football chant.

"

On writing "We are the Champions", *Circus* magazine, 19 January 1978

“

We're gonna stay together until we fucking well die, I'm sure of it. I keep – I must tell you – I keep wanting to leave, but they won't let me. Also, I suppose we're not... We're not bad for four aging queens, are we? Really, what do you think?

”

Live at Wembley, shortly before performing "Who Wants to Live Forever", 1986

Top Five Queen Songs

1. Bohemian Rhapsody (1975)

It officially became the most streamed song of all time in December 2018.

2. Don't Stop Me Now (1978)

Its use in several successful movies has pushed this track to the top of the charts.

3. Under Pressure (1981)

This immensely successful collaboration with David Bowie reached number one in the UK.

4. Another One Bites the Dust (1980)

Written by John Deacon, the groundbreaking hit spent 15 weeks in the Billboard top 10.

5. We Will Rock You (1977)

Written by Brian May, the anthem was inducted into the Grammy Hall of Fame in 2009.

"

In the beginning I was quite prepared to starve, which I did, and just make a go of it. You have to believe in yourself, no matter how long it takes.

"

As quoted in an article on recordcollectormag.com, 15 October 2007

66

If he didn't have the music, he wouldn't have lasted.

99

Freddie's long-term partner, Jim Hutton, as quoted in "Queen's Tragic Rhapsody", *Rolling Stone*, 7 July 2014

"

In the end, I mean I just took the plunge and I said that's exactly what I want to do, and I think that's the only way to approach this business… you can't sort of do it in half measures, you really can't…

"

Interview with Simon Bates, BBC Radio 1, June 1985

"

It's so easy to be trodden on, that you have to be hardened to the fact very early on… It's like playing dodgems really, it's rock 'n' roll dodgems… and, and the higher up the ladder you go, the more problems you get and the harder it becomes… I'm not sort of asking for sympathy or anything, I'm just saying that's what it's all about.

"

Interview with Simon Bates, BBC Radio 1, June 1985

66

Do you know, it's not... very often that we do shows in daylight. And I fucking wish we'd done before, I can see you all now. And there's some beauties here tonight, I can tell you!

99

Live at Milton Keynes Bowl, UK, 5 June 1982

> **"**
> I'm going into opera, forget
> rock 'n' roll!
> **"**

Final interview, conducted by Rudi Dolezal, speaking of
his collaboration with Montserrat Caballé, early 1987

At some point in every Queen performance, Freddie sang into a "bottomless mic" without a stand.

The origins of that gimmick were accidental – at an early Queen performance, Freddie was in the middle of performing when his mic stand broke. Instead of grabbing another one, he continued singing – and liked it so much, it became a trademark.

66

I like people to go away
from a Queen show feeling
fully entertained, having
had a good time.

99

"The Man Who Would Be Queen", *Melody Maker*,
2 May 1981

CHAPTER
FOUR

KILLER QUEEN

Freddie, the Style Icon...

The name Freddie Mercury is
synonymous with flamboyance. Wearing
everything from glittering catsuits to
military-style jackets studded with
epaulettes – and famously dressing up
as a repressed housewife, in a leather
mini skirt and dangling earrings for the
"I Want to Break Free" video – the
Queen frontman was never afraid
to break the rules.

"

Killer Queen was one song which was really out of the format that I usually write in. Usually, the music comes first, but the words came to me, and the sophisticated style that I wanted to put across in the song, came first. No, I'd never really met a woman like that. A lot of my songs are fantasy.

"

In an interview with Caroline Coon, "The Queen Bee", *Melody Maker*, 21 December 1974

66

I used to go home periodically
and turn up in these outrageous
clothes, with my fingernails
painted black, and at that time
my mother used to freak out!
They used to say, 'My God!
Don't let the neighbours see
you. Come in here quick!
Use the back door!'

99

Freddie Mercury: A Life, In His Own Words,
September 2019

Freddie had a love of ballet, and in 1979, he agreed to make a cameo at a charity gala for the Royal Ballet in London.

Performing with professional dancers, he sang "Bohemian Rhapsody" and "Crazy Little Thing Called Love" at the London Coliseum in front of 2,500 people.

"

I wear my ballet shoes every time I write.

"

Interview, 1977

"

Killer Queen I wrote in one night. I'm not being conceited or anything, but it just fell into place. Certain songs do.

"

In an interview with Caroline Coon, "The Queen Bee", *Melody Maker*, 21 December 1974

66

I look back at myself, and think oh my God, how could I have done that, wearing black nail varnish, the long hair and the make-up... but everybody grows out of it.

99

Radio 1990, February 1984

> 66
>
> I could cause a riot if
> I wanted to but I still think
> that's a minor matter
> because it's all very tongue-
> in-cheek…
>
> 99

"The Man Who Would Be Queen", *Melody Maker*,
2 May 1981

" I like to ridicule myself.
I don't take it too seriously.
I wouldn't wear these
clothes if I was serious. **"**

"The Man Who Would Be Queen", *Melody Maker*,
2 May 1981

"
Gay as a daffodil.

"

As quoted by Julie Webb for *New Musical Express*,
12 March 1974

66

I love posing. That's for the press.

99

Live in concert at Earl's Court, London, 1977

In 1980, "Crazy Little Thing Called Love" was written by Freddie in just 10 minutes after dreaming up the song in a bubble bath in a Munich hotel. It topped the charts in the US, where it remained for four weeks, and the Australian charts, where it remained at number one for seven weeks.

Freddie performed the song live playing rhythm guitar – the first time he played guitar in concert with Queen.

66

I fall in love far too quickly and end up getting hurt all the time. I've got scars all over. But I can't help myself because basically I'm a softie I have this hard, macho shell – which I project on stage but there's a much softer side. too, which melts like butter.

99

As quoted in "Rock on, Freddie", *Sunday Magazine*, May 1985

> **"**
> I hate pockets in trousers...
> By the way, I do not wear a
> hose. My hose is my own.
> No coke bottle, nothing
> stuffed down there.
> **"**

NME, 2 November 1974

66

I play better piano with my right hand than I do with my left. There's more things I don't do with my left hand than I do with my right. I'll tell you one thing, I only wear nail polish on my left hand. It's the only hand I'll wear black nail polish on. I only need it on one hand.

99

"Queen's Freddie Mercury Shopping for an Image in London", *Circus Magazine*, April 1975

Five Iconic Outfits

Madison Square Garden, 1977
Sequined jumpsuit with a plunging v-neckline
and a white mask.

Queen's UK tour, 1978
All-black PVC leather outfit with a jacket
embellished with plastic patches. Teamed with
a black hat and dark sunglasses.

Queen's "It's a Hard Life" video, 1984
Red "prawn suit" designed by Natasha Korniloff,
featuring eyes splayed across the bright fabric.

Live Aid, Wembley Stadium, 1985
White tank top teamed with denim jeans and
a studded belt and armband.

Wembley Stadium, 1986
Yellow belted jacket with gold buckles, eyelets
and trim. Paired with white trousers with a red
stripe down either leg, embellished with gold.

66
I dress to kill, but tastefully.
99

Article by Emma Powys Maurice, posted on thepinknews.com, 24 November 2021

66
Dullness is a disease.

99

Article by Daniel Welsh, posted on huffingtonpost.co.uk,
24 November 2021

66

I often wonder what my mother must think when she sees way-out pictures of me on stage in all that regalia and make up. But like my father, she doesn't ask any questions.

99

As quoted in an article on recordcollectormag.com, 15 October 2007

66

I like to be surrounded
by splendid things. I want
to lead the Victorian
life, surrounded by
exquisite clutter.

99

As quoted in an article on recordcollectormag.com,
15 October 2007

66

Some of my best clothes are [antique]. They're the clothes I like best. I don't like manufactured clothes.

99

"Queen's Freddie Mercury Shopping for an Image in London", *Circus Magazine*, April 1975

In 1982, the disco-oriented album *Hot Space* divided both critics and hardcore fans.

The 1984 album, *The Works*, did much better, though the video for "I Want to Break Free" – which saw Freddie and his bandmates dressed in full drag – did not go down well in the US, and had a lasting impact on the band's reputation there.

"

I think ['I Want to Break Free'
is] one of our best videos to
date, really, in fact it still makes
me chuckle every time I see it...
Everybody thinks it probably was
my idea... but the funny thing
is the others came up with the
idea and I said 'Fine, I'll do it.'

"

On dressing up in drag for the "I Want to Break Free"
video, interview with Simon Bates, BBC Radio 1,
June 1985

66

At the moment, I don't have any [money]. I spend it as soon as I get it, on a house, clothes, paintings. I love going to restaurants and spending money on good food.

99

"Queen's Freddie Mercury Shopping for an Image in London", *Circus Magazine*, April 1975

66

Highly Strung? We fight over hairspray!

99

As quoted in *NME*, 27 April 1974

66

Of all the more theatrical performers, Freddie took it further than the rest. He took it over the edge. And of course I always admire a man who wears tights!

99

David Bowie, as quoted on brianmay.com, 5 September 2015

66

I like buying things on crazy impulses. I hate buying for investment. But I do like a lot of Oriental stuff; it's intricate and delicate. I also like the cultural part of it, the way they do their gardens; they put a lot of thought into it.

99

On Japanese style, after playing shows in Tokyo, Japan, *Rolling Stone*, 11 June 1981

66

Here you are, after
13 years, four old ladies
are still rocking away.

99

Interview, Munich, 1984

"

From now on, dressing up
crazily on stage is out.
I don't think a 42-year-old
man should be running
around in a leotard any more.
It's not very becoming.

"

As quoted in an article on recordcollectormag.com,
15 October 2007

In the 1980s, Freddie lived in Munich for several years. For his 39th birthday, he threw a legendary party for 300 friends at Old Mrs Henderson, a famous cabaret bar.

It was a night of true excess involving horse-drawn carriages, black and white drag and a 1.5 metre- (5 foot-) high champagne fountain.

❝

It was one of the more
outrageous parties that I
have ever attended. I don't
think there was one like
it afterwards.

❞

Freddie's personal assistant, Peter "Phoebe" Freestone,
describing Freddie Mercury's 39th birthday party in
Munich, 1985

CHAPTER
FIVE

A KIND OF MAGIC

Freddie, the Showman...

Freddie Mercury's talent as a singer and songwriter is undisputed, but he was equally admired for his magnetic stage presence and charisma.

He had a unique ability to captivate and engage his audience with his electrifying performances. Connecting with his fans on an emotional level, the star conveyed a sense of disarming vulnerability and authenticity that continues to resonate with us today.

"

I thought up the name Queen early on. It couldn't have been King; it doesn't have the same ring or aura as Queen. It was a very regal name and it sounded splendid. It's strong, very universal, and immediate. It had a lot of visual potential and was open to all sorts of interpretations.

"

As quoted in "Queen's Tragic Rhapsody", *Rolling Stone*, 7 July 2014

"

I feel that the name Queen actually fitted that time. It lent itself to a lot of things, like the theatre, and it was grand. It was very pompous, with all kinds of connotations. It meant so much. It wasn't just one precise label.

"

Article by Emma Powys Maurice, posted on thepinknews.com, 24 November 2021

Given Freddie's songwriting talent and undeniable star power, it might seem surprising that he didn't fully step out as a solo artist until 1984.

His first proper solo single was "Love Kills", written for the new soundtrack of Giorgio Moroder's restoration of Fritz Lang's 1927 silent cinema classic *Metropolis*.

"

I hate doing the same thing again and again and again. I like to see what's happening now in music, film and theatre and incorporate all of those things.

"

Interview, 1986

❝

I just like having fun. It's a very good release, rock music, but you know you say that I am a different person on stage and that same thing could be said of anyone going out to do his job.

❞

"The Man Who Would Be Queen", *Melody Maker*, 2 May 1981

"

I'm so powerful on stage that I seem to have created a monster. When I'm performing, I'm an extrovert, yet inside I'm a completely different man.

"

As quoted in "Rock on, Freddie", *Sunday Magazine*, May 1985

> **66**
>
> I love the fact that I can make people happy, in any form. Even if it's just an hour of their lives, if I can make them feel lucky or make them feel good, or bring a smile to a sour face, that to me is worthwhile.
>
> **99**

Article by Daniel Welsh, posted on huffingtonpost.co.uk, 24 November 2021

> **"**
> The most important thing is
> to live a fabulous life. As
> long as it's fabulous I don't
> care how long it is.
> **"**

Article by Emma Powys Maurice, posted on
thepinknews.com, 24 November 2021

Freddie dedicated his first solo album, *Mr Bad Guy*, to "my cat Jerry – also Tom, Oscar and Tiffany, and all the cat lovers across the universe – screw everybody else."

The Queen frontman was renowned for his love of cats, often calling to speak to them from the road. The song "Delilah", from the 1991 album *Innuendo*, is about his cat.

66

I'm leaving it all to Mary and the cats.

99

Talking about his will, in one of his final interviews with journalist David Wigg

❝

I have to win people over,
otherwise it's not a
successful gig. It's my job
to make sure people have a
good time. That's part of
my duty. It's all to do with
feeling in control.

❞

The Sun, 19 July 1985

66

A concert is not a live rendition of our album. It's a theatrical event.

99

Circus magazine, 17 March 1977

66

The reason we're successful, darling? My overall charisma, of course.

99

Article by Daniel Welsh, posted on huffingtonpost.co.uk, 24 November 2021

66

We fought on virtually the first day... we used to fight about musical ideas, and this and that... we all have egos... but the fighting seems to keep us together.

99

Interview, Munich, 1984

"

If I'm dead and I want to be buried with all my treasures, like Tutankhamen, I'll do it. If I want a pyramid in Kensington, and I can afford it, I'll have it. Wouldn't that be fab? Will I get to heaven? No. I don't want to. Hell is much better. Look at all the interesting people you're going to meet down there!

"

As quoted in an article on recordcollectormag.com, 15 October 2007

66

The Carmen Miranda of rock & roll."

99

Commenting on his stage persona, "Queen Holds Court in South America", *Rolling Stone*, 11 June 1981

On 13 July 1985, Queen – and Freddie in particular – gave an electrifying performance at Live Aid. In the 20-minute set at London's Wembley Stadium, the singer commanded the stage and held the 72,000-strong crowd in the palm of his hand.

Watched by an estimated 1.9 billion people on TV around the world, Freddie's legendary performance has gone down in history as one of the best ever.

Ay-Oh!

Freddie's improvised call to the Live Aid crowd,
showing his unique ability to interact with and win over
a huge audience, 13 July 1985

❝

That was entirely down to Freddie. The rest of us played OK, but Freddie was out there and took it to another level.

❞

Brian May commenting on Freddie's electric performance at Live Aid, 13 July 1985

66

After the first five years when we had the taste of success, that's the time where I thought oh my God, I was the bees knees and I mean nobody could speak to me, and I couldn't be seen in these places, but you learn to live with it, and afterwards you realize that it's also growing up and getting experience, and now I think I'm not afraid to go anywhere…

99

Saturday Live with Graham Neale, *The Works* album, BBC Radio 1, 15 September 1984

Freddie first met hairdresser Jim Hutton at a London gay club in 1985. Eighteen months later, they began a relationship that would last for the rest of the singer's life.

While they never married (same-sex marriage was still illegal at that time), they both wore a wedding ring to show their commitment to each other. Hutton cared for Freddie after his AIDS diagnosis and was present at his bedside when he died in 1991.

66

I'm possessed by love – but isn't everybody? Most of my songs are love ballads and things to do with sadness and torture and pain.

99

As quoted in "I am the Champion" by Nick Ferrari, *The Sun*, 19 July 1985

"

I'm a bit of everything... in the public eye, you see, what's been put across, of course, is my stage persona, which is very arrogant, very aggressive, or whatever... and whenever people want to talk about me, or when they see me in public, they're attuned to what they see and they just think I'm arrogant or whatever, and, and in one way that's nice, because I don't want everyone to know about my real inner feelings, because that's my private life...

"

Interview with Simon Bates, BBC Radio 1, June 1985

66

I don't want to change the
world with our music. There
are no hidden messages
in our songs, except for
some of Brian's.

99

"The Man Who Would Be Queen", in *Melody Maker*,
2 May 1981

66

What you must understand is that my voice comes from the energy of the audience. The better they are, the better I get.

99

As quoted in "Queen's Tragic Rhapsody",
Rolling Stone, 7 July 2014

66

Well, I don't ever really sit down at the piano and say, 'Right, I've got to write a song now.' I feel a few things and I have ideas. It's very hard to explain but there are always various ideas going through my head.

99

In an interview with Caroline Coon, "The Queen Bee", *Melody Maker*, 21 December 1974

Freddie adored opera, and in 1986, he playfully said on Spanish TV that the soprano Montserrat Caballé was his favourite singer. When Caballé was asked to produce a theme song for the 1992 Barcelona Olympic games, she asked Freddie to collaborate with her. The result was the iconic recording of "Barcelona" and album by the same name.

The song was performed live in Barcelona in October 1988, at the open-air La Nit festival. This was the last live performance by Freddie, who was already beginning to suffer from AIDS.

"

While he was singing, I noticed that his eyes were shiny with tears. I gave him my hand. He clasped it and kissed it. It was clear he was suddenly aware of his own fate. They were tears of farewell. It was his goodbye, at least to the stage.

"

Montserrat Caballé recalls her 1988 live performance with Freddie in Barcelona, in an interview with Spencer Bright

"

Thanks to me
[Montserrat Caballé] has
become a rocker.

"

As quoted in "How Freddie Mercury and
Montserrat Caballé made musical history", *El País*,
8 October 2018

"

[Freddie and Montserrat Caballé] had arranged to have lunch at 1pm. In his suite, Freddie was chain-smoking and pacing… Then this crowded lobby parted like the red sea and Montserrat walked through. She said later she was so happy because, when she took Fred's hand, it was colder than hers, which meant he was even more nervous than she was.

"

Freddie's PA Peter Freestone describes the charged first meeting between the singer and Montserrat Caballé, *NME*, 25 October 2019

CHAPTER
SIX

THE SHOW MUST GO ON

Fame, Fortune and Fate...

Freddie was diagnosed with AIDS in 1987, but despite his deteriorating health, he continued to write and record music. One of the standout tracks of the album *Innuendo* is "The Show Must Go On", written by Brian May.

Freddie gave his all in the recording studio and the song has since become a beloved classic – and a testament to Freddie's unique talent, star quality and resilience.

"

We finished the British tour last night and I feel as if I've done a marathon every night. I've got bruises everywhere.

"

In an interview with Caroline Coon, "The Queen Bee", *Melody Maker*, 21 December 1974

66

Quite often I have quite vicious nightmares – like the other night just before the Rainbow concert. We were sleeping in the Holiday Inn and I dreamed I went out on to the hotel balcony and the whole thing fell and I was a heap on the pavement. Really, I was petrified when I woke up in the morning.

99

In an interview with Caroline Coon, "The Queen Bee", *Melody Maker*, 21 December 1974

"

I don't want to keep playing
the same formula over
and over again, otherwise
you just go insane. I don't
want to become stale.
I want to be creative.

"

NME, June 1977

66

I'm a big ham really. I just get on stage and do it. I don't really take myself that seriously anymore.

99

Interview with *Entertainment Tonight*, 1982

“

Why kill the goose that laid the golden egg?

”

On Queen staying together for more than a decade, interview with David Wigg, 1985

66

This next song is only dedicated to beautiful people here tonight. That means all of you. Thank you for coming along... and making this a great occasion.

99

Live Aid, 13 July 1985

"

You bastards, you stole
the show!

"

Elton John to Queen backstage at Live Aid, following
Freddie's stellar performance, 13 July 1985

❝
When my legs give out,
I'll be happy to just sit
around in bandages,
knitting socks for sailors!
❞

As quoted in an article on recordcollectormag.com,
15 October 2007

Freddie was diagnosed with AIDS in 1987, although he may have displayed symptoms as early as 1982.

Although the star did his best to keep his illness private, his increasingly gaunt appearance – especially at the 1990 Brit Awards, when all four Queen members came on stage to collect the award For Outstanding Contribution – caused intense media speculation.

On 23 November 1991, a statement issued to the press confirmed Freddie's diagnosis. Less than 24 hours later, the Queen frontman was dead.

"

Freddie had a fairly peaceful night as though a weight had been lifted from his shoulders... I have never seen him so relaxed because the secret was out. There was nothing to hide. He had stopped taking his medication and he was prepared.

"

Peter Freestone, Freddie's PA, recalling the singer's demeanour following the press release announcing his AIDS diagnosis, as quoted in *The Big Issue*, 3 October 2021

66

If I'm seen to be having fun onstage, I think it comes across... I couldn't get any more theatrical, I just think that's the way I want to perform. It's grasping a song and delivering it the way I feel is right.

99

Interview with *Entertainment Tonight*, 1982

"
Will my music stand the test of time? I don't give a fuck. I won't be around to worry about it. In 20 years' time… I'll be dead darling. Are you mad?

"

As quoted in an article on recordcollectormag.com, 15 October 2007

"

It could all end tomorrow. I'm not afraid of it. It's a precarious life but I think I like it that way. I like it a little risky. Okay, so I'm quite well off but money in the bank doesn't mean anything to me. I spend it as quickly as it comes. I could be penniless tomorrow, but I wouldn't care that much. I have this survival instinct in me.

"

"The Man Who Would Be Queen", *Melody Maker*, 2 May 1981

66

I'm losing the range [of my voice], believe it or not. I've lost the power I began with. But I've become a stronger singer so maybe my framework is diminishing but within that I can sing better than ever. My voice can do amazing things now.

99

On his voice, "The Man Who Would Be Queen", *Melody Maker*, 2 May 1981

Although he wasn't well enough to tour, Freddie continued to record with Queen until shortly before his death.

The final album released in Freddie's lifetime, *Innuendo*, was released in 1991. His final track, "A Winter Tale", was written in Switzerland, and inspired by staring out of windows in various places in Montreux, including from his hospital bed in Lake Geneva.

Freddie was posthumously featured on the band's final album, *Made in Heaven* (1995).

"

It's hard to describe what happened during those final days. All Fred's troubles were left outside the studio. We became an incredibly close-knit family.

"

Brian May on Freddie's final days in the recording studio, *Mojo*, 2019

"

Darling, my attitude is 'fuck it'. I'm doing everything with everybody.

"

On being asked, in 1984, if the fear of AIDS had changed his behaviour, as quoted in "Queen's Tragic Rhapsody", *Rolling Stone*, 7 July 2014

> **"**
> I don't want to change the world. To me, happiness is the most important thing. If I'm happy, it shows in my work.
> **"**

Final filmed interview, with Rudi Dolezal, early 1987

"

You can play good when you're struggling and I think you can play good when you've made it, as well... I mean, when I go on stage, whether I'm rich or starving, I want to give my all. I want to go on there and die for the show!

"

"The Man Who Would Be Queen", *Melody Maker*, 2 May 1981

"

When I can't sing anymore darling, then I will die.

"

As recalled by Brian May's wife, Anita Dobson, BBC documentary *Freddie Mercury: The Final Act*, 2021

66

Interviewer: "What, what drives you on, I mean you're rich, you're famous, and you don't need to work. What drives you on?"

Mercury: "At this very moment it's two wonderful names... and that is Montserrat Caballé."

"

Interview with David Wigg, 1987

"

I don't expect to make old bones, and what's more I don't really care. I certainly don't have any aspirations to live to 70. It would be so boring. I will be dead and gone long before that. I'll be starting a new life somewhere else, growing my own pomegranates.

"

As quoted in an article on recordcollectormag.com, 15 October 2007

"

The first time we really knew was when we got together in Montreux. Freddie just sat down and said 'OK, you guys probably know what is going on with me. You know what I am dealing with. I don't want to talk about it.'

"

Brian May recalls the moment Freddie revealed his AIDS diagnosis, BBC documentary *Freddie Mercury: The Final Act*, 2021

On 20 April 1992, The Freddie Mercury Tribute Concert for AIDS awareness was held at London's Wembley Stadium.

The star-studded line-up included George Michael and Queen singing "Someone to Love" and Annie Lennox and David Bowie singing "Under Pressure".

The profits were used to launch the Mercury Phoenix Trust, to fight HIV/AIDS worldwide.

FREDDIE MERCURY

66

Good evening Wembley
and the world. We are here
tonight to celebrate the
life, and work, and dreams,
of one Freddie Mercury.
We're gonna give him the
biggest send-off in history!

99

Brian May addressing the crowd at the Freddie Mercury
Tribute Concert, 20 April 1992

"

As far as we are concerned, this is it. There is no point carrying on. It is impossible to replace Freddie.

"

John Deacon in the aftermath of Freddie's death, 1991

66

I have never got over his death.
None of us have. I think that we
all thought that we could come
to terms with it quite quickly, but
we underestimated the impact his
death had on our lives. I still find
it difficult to talk about. For those
of us left, it is as though Queen
was another lifetime entirely.

99

Roger Taylor, as quoted in "Queen's Tragic Rhapsody",
Rolling Stone, 7 July 2014

66

As far as I'm concerned,
I really have lived a full life,
and if I'm dead tomorrow,
I don't give a damn. I live,
you know, I really have done
it all, I really have.

99

Interview with David Wigg, 1987